The Kids' TabLe

by Colleen Madden

One Christmas ...

... a girl who was eight
and tall for her years,
with good taste in clothes
and jewels in her ears,
was told to sit at the kids' table.

Not quite a teen
but no longer a tot,
she wondered why the adults
hadn't saved her a spot.

So there she sat, like a little kid,
with a bowl and a spoon
and a cup with a lid.

"Is this for real?"
the girl asked out loud.
"Why am I stuck
with this babyish crowd?"

Then her cousin Billy
poured slop on her thigh.
She glared round the dining room,
trying not to cry.

"This ISN'T FAIR! This ISN'T cool!
To make me spend Christmas
with kids who still drool!"

The girl jumped up from her chair
and started to shout.
"If this is a joke,
YOU'D BETTER CUT IT RIGHT OUT!

If you think I eat mush
then I'm really offended.
Unlike these toddlers,
I don't eat my food blended!"

"In maths, I can do a four-figure sum,
and I earned my swimming badge
last summer with Mum.
I make my own pancakes.
I can microwave!
I can sit at the big table.
I know how to behave!"

"I KNOW
how to use
a fork!

I KNOW HOW TO USE A KNIFE!"

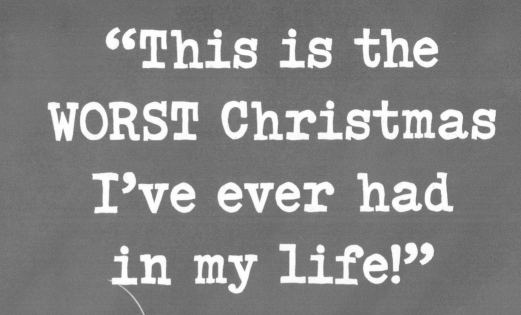

"This is the WORST Christmas I've ever had in my life!"

I DESERVE A PLACE AT THE ADULT TABLE!

SHLOOOOOOOP!

The quiet was loud,
but Mum saved the day.
Thankfully mums always
know what to say.

"You're too old to sit with babies.
I see what you mean.
You are at a tough age.
You're stuck in between.

Next time please ask me
if you'd rather sit with us.
Don't yell across the room
and create such a fuss.

I'll clear you a space
at the dining room table.
Calm down and clean up,
and sit down when you're able."

Dinner was served
with the best plates and glasses.
The girl told her cousin
about her dance classes.

After dinner's end,
her parents got a huge hug and a kiss.
For she felt like a grown-up,
a big girl's one wish!

She helped wash the dishes,
she put things away.
Then she waved to the babies
at the end of the day.

She said goodbye,
feeling just a bit sad.
For as Christmases go,
this one wasn't so bad.